Animal Antics

Animal Antics

A Cat Record Book

JUDY REINEN
with RICHARD STACKS

hAVoc
PUBLISHING INC.

Contents

Contents

My Arrival

My name is

....

I was born on

....

There were .... kittens in my litter

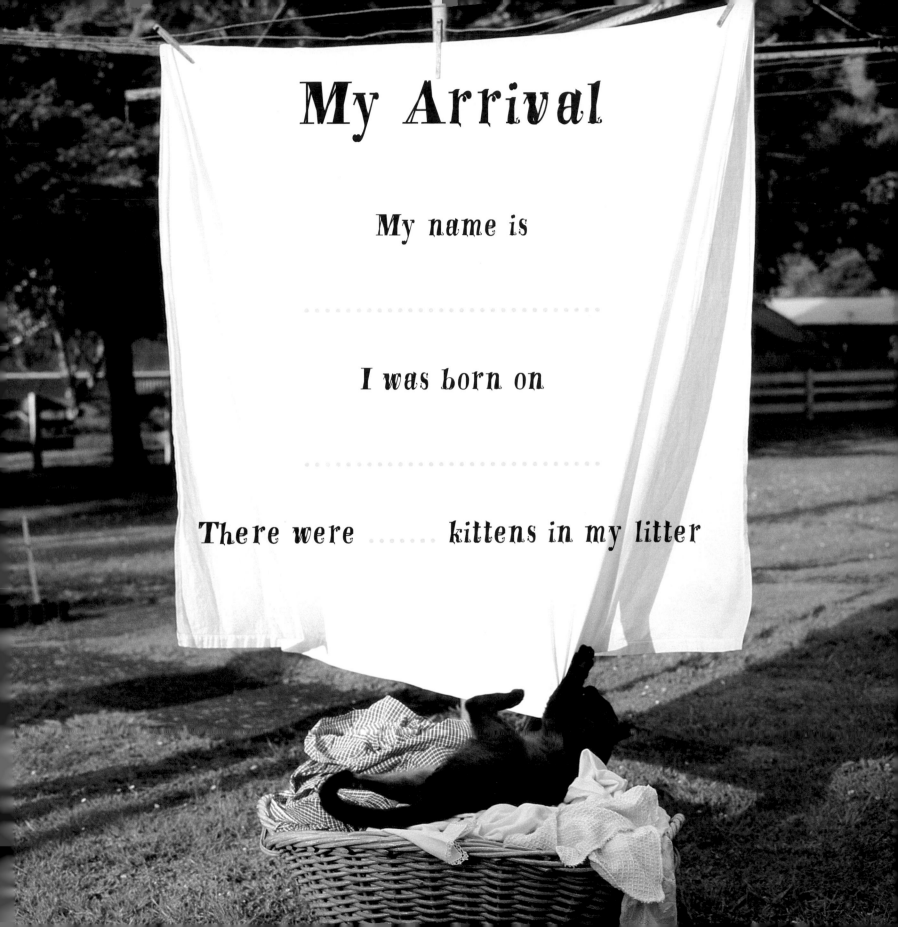

My Name

I am called ....

My other names are

....

My Breed

I am a

....

We are known for

....

....

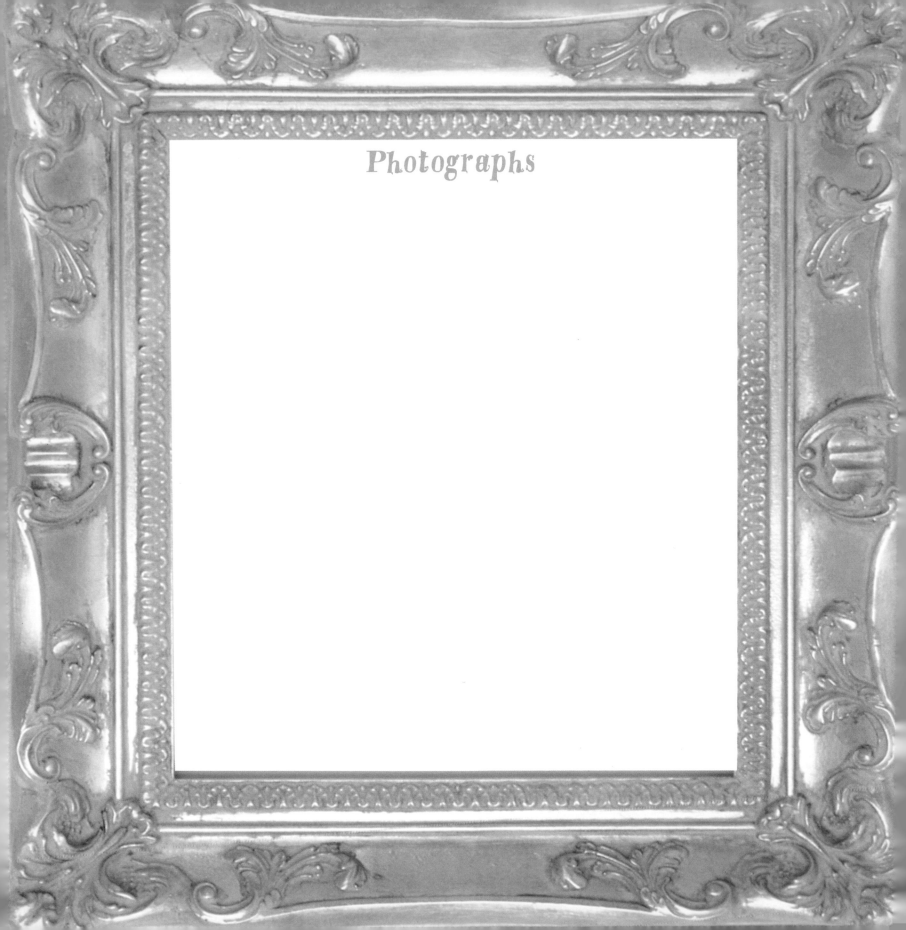

Photographs

Photographs

Best Features

My eyes are

My paws are

My whiskers are

My ears are

Lineage

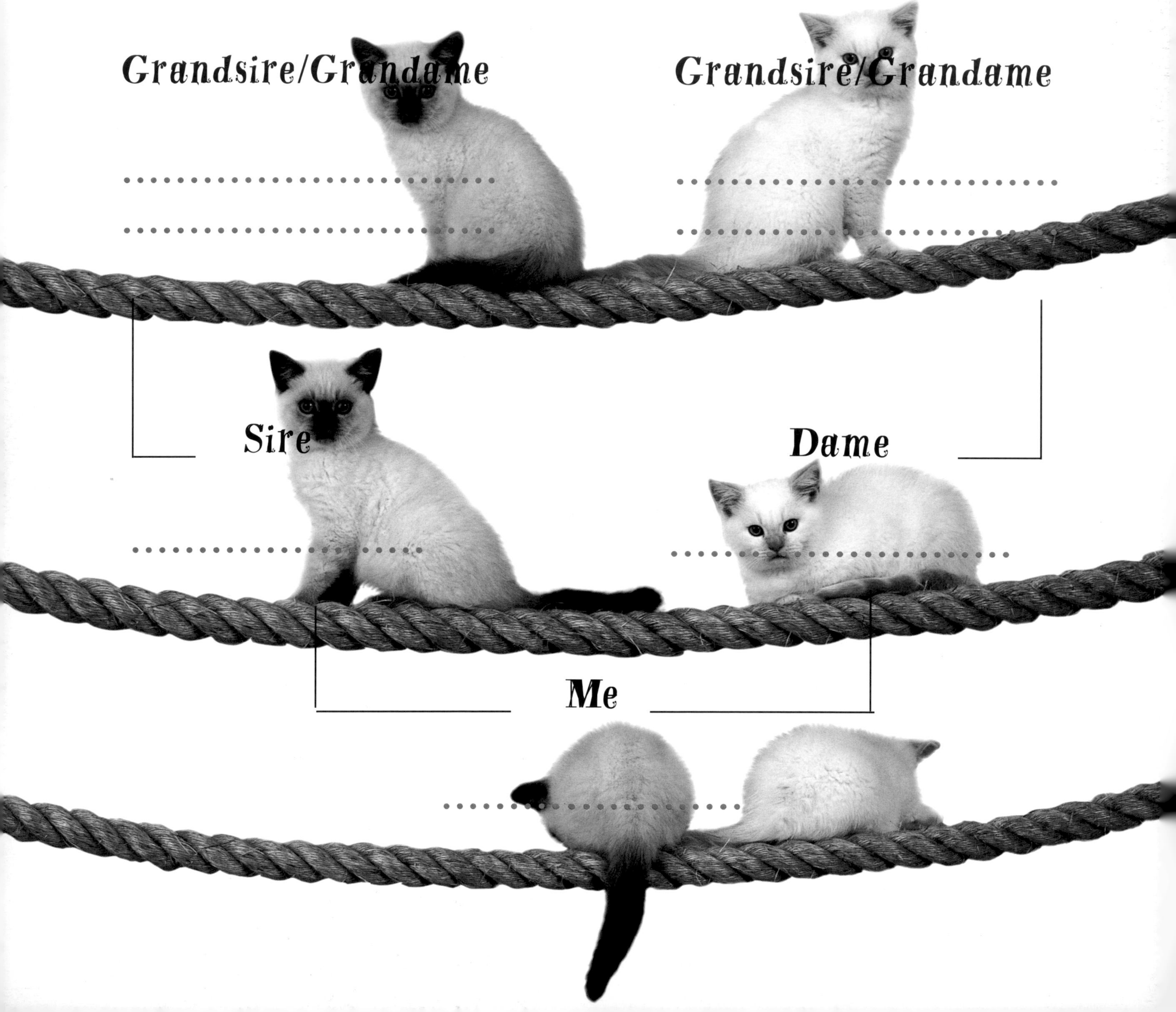

Grandsire/Grandame

·····································

·····································

Grandsire/Grandame

·····································

·····································

Sire

·····································

Dame

·····································

Me

·····································

My Family

My owner is ....

We live at ....

Family members ....

Other relatives ....

Neighbours ....

Photographs

Photographs

Growing Up

Birthdays

Year . . . .

For a present I got . . . .

Party guests . . . .

Year . . . .

For a present I got . . . .

Party guests . . . .

Birthdays

Year ....

For a present I got ....

Party guests ....

Year ....

For a present I got ....

Party guests ....

Birthdays

Year ....

For a present I got ....

Party guests ....

Year ....

For a present I got ....

Party guests ....

Photographs

Photographs

Christmas

Year ....

For a present I got ....

Christmas dinner ....

Year ....

For a present I got ....

Christmas dinner ....

Christmas

Year ....

For a present I got ....

Christmas dinner ....

Year ....

For a present I got ....

Christmas dinner ....

Year ....

For a present I got ....

Christmas dinner ....

Christmas

Year ....

For a present I got ....

Christmas dinner ....

Year ....

For a present I got ....

Christmas dinner ....

Photographs

Photographs

Outings

Special events

· ·

· ·

· ·

· ·

· ·

Destinations

· ·

· ·

· ·

· ·

· ·

Best Friends

My best friends are   Our favourite games are

Favourite Food

Favourite Pastimes

Photographs

Photographs

Holidays

....

....

....

....

....

....

Gone Fishing

Great Catches

Adventures

Favourite Spots

Favourite Spots

Photographs

Photographs

Achievements

Great things I have done

· ·

· ·

· ·

· ·

· ·

· ·

Exercise

....

....

....

....

....

....

Grooming

Record

Flea Treatments

Date   Date   Date

Photographs

Photographs

Visits to the Vet

Date	Illness	Treatment

Vaccination

Date	Vaccine
....	....
....	....
....	....
....	....
....	....
....	....
....	....
....	....
....	....
....	....

Worming

Worm Treatments

Date	Date	Date	Date	Date

Important Addresses

Name ....

Address ....

....

Phone ....

Name ....

Address ....

....

Phone ....

Name ....

Address ....

....

Phone ....

Name ....

Address ....

....

Phone ....

Name ....

Address ....

....

Phone ....

Name ....

Address ....

....

Phone ....

Judy Reinen has had a camera in her hands from an early age. Following in her father's footsteps, Judy started Creative Shotz Photography in Auckland, New Zealand, where she has built a reputation for unique wedding and portrait photography.

Judy loves animals and is passionate about photographing them. She

owns a blue-point Persian cat called Yabba Dabba Doo, who "purrs so loudly his nickname is Tractor", an adventurous tortoise-shell Persian called Pancake and a Tibetan terrier named Basil.

"It has been such a pleasure to photograph each dog and cat. I'm constantly sidetracked. I want to cuddle them all. Each dog and cat has been a star and loved all the fuss. After my Great Dane, Major, passed away, I wished that I had a complete record of his life. I decided to make a series of Record Books so that everyone can have a lifetime of memories of their special friends."

Judy has won numerous international awards, including the prestigious Master of Photography title from the NZ Institute of Professional Photography.

Titles available in the *Animal Antics* series:
Cat Record Book
Dog Record Book
Cat Address & Telephone Book (two formats)
Dog Address & Telephone Book (two formats)

ISBN 1-57977-005-3

Contents © 1996 Creative Shotz Limited
Selected images © Richard Stacks as provided by Cedco Publishing,
2955 Kerner Blvd, San Rafael, CA 94901, U.S.A.

ANIMAL ANTICS ™

Published in 1997 by Havoc Publishing Inc.
7868 Silverton Avenue, Suite A
San Diego, California, USA 92126

For further information on other Animal Antics products, please write to us.

Design by Trevor Newman
Printed through Bookbuilders, Hong Kong